Perspectives

Thinking Outside the Box

What Does It Mean?

Series Consultant: Linda Hoyt

Flying Start
to Literacy®

Contents

Introduction   4

It's only natural   6

Speak out!   10

Accidental inventions   12

A clever solution   14

How to write about your opinion   16

Introduction

How do people solve problems?
How do they invent new things?

Most people who invent something new think in an original or creative way – they think outside the box.

Some have luck on their side, and create or invent things by accident. Some get their ideas by observing nature. Most are determined and keep persisting until they get it "just right". And all these problem solvers use the knowledge that people have been building upon for thousands of years.

Think of a problem you have solved. How did you do it?

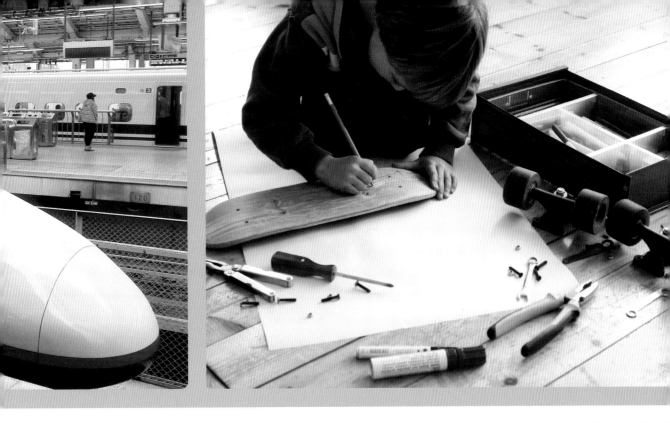

It's only natural

Many of the things we use every day were inspired by the way things work in nature. People have copied from nature to invent things we use all the time.

Why do you think scientists, inventors and designers observe and study animals and plants for inspiration?

People got the idea of
flight from birds.

Ducks' webbed feet
inspired flippers.

Sticky burrs sparked
the idea for Velcro.

The idea for
suction cups
came from
the octopus.

Speak out!

Read what these students have to say about solving problems and thinking outside the box.

It's good to use your imagination. You get so many more ideas if you think creatively.

If you want to solve problems, you have to think outside the box – you can't just follow what everyone else does.

Sometimes, you shouldn't think outside the box. If you are following a map, you might end up going the wrong way if you think outside the box.

My best ideas come when I work with someone else. At school, we work in teams, so it can get a bit noisy, but I think that's okay.

I like solving problems by myself. I find it really challenging, but a challenge is good for your brain.

Accidental inventions

Did you know that some of the most popular things we use today were invented accidentally? Why do you think these accidental inventions became popular?

Potato chips

An unhappy diner complained to the chef that his fried potatoes were too thick. The chef cut them thinner, but the diner complained that they were still too thick.

The chef was annoyed, so he cut the next batch as thin as he could, and the diner loved them! These were the first potato chips.

Popsicles

An 11-year-old boy put a stick
in a cup of soda water and left
it on his porch overnight in
the middle of winter.
The next morning, the
mixture was frozen.
This was the first Popsicle.

Sticky notes

Sticky notes – we use them every day. But did you
know that they were an accidental invention? A
chemist was trying to make a superstrong glue, but
the glue ended up superweak. He didn't know what to
do with his invention.

But someone who worked with the
chemist did! He attached some of
the weak glue to bookmarks to stop
them falling out of his books. It
worked, and today sticky notes
are used all around the world.

A clever solution

Written by Maria Hlohowskyj

Why do birds fly into windows? Do they have trouble seeing them?

Alfred Arnold is a bird lover who wanted to help fix this problem. As Arnold worked on the problem, what special skills did he use?

Arnold also happened to own a glass company. He was so concerned about the birds, he wondered if he could make a glass window that was see-through to humans but looked solid to birds.

Arnold used what he knew about how birds see light to invent a special type of glass. This glass is covered in a web pattern that birds can see, but humans can't. To humans, the glass looks clear. But to birds, it looks like a net.

Arnold's new glass is being used in many buildings. The glass costs a bit more, but it could save thousands of birds from crashing into windows and injuring or killing themselves.

As scientists learn more about how birds see, they might come up with even better ideas.

How to write about your opinion

State your opinion

Think about the main question in the introduction on page 4 of this book. What is your opinion?

Research

Look for other information that you need to back up your opinion.

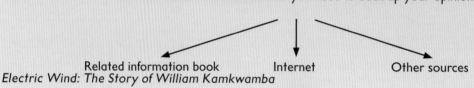

Related information book
Electric Wind: The Story of William Kamkwamba   Internet   Other sources

Make a plan

Introduction

How will you "hook" the reader to get them interested?

Write a sentence that makes your opinion clear.

List reasons to support your opinion.

Support your reason
with examples.   Support your reason
with examples.   Support your reason
with examples.

Conclusion

Write a sentence that makes your opinion clear. Leave your reader with a strong message.

Publish

Publish your writing.

Include some graphics or visual images.

Don't Throw It Away!

Written by Lee Wang
Series Consultant: Linda Hoyt

WorldWise™
Content-based Learning

Contents

Introduction 3

**Chapter 1: What's the problem
                with rubbish? 4**
Are you the problem? 4
Our space is limited 5
Our resources are limited 9

Chapter 2: People taking action 10
Reduce 10
Reuse 12
Recycle 14

Chapter 3: What can you do? 16
At home: Inside 16
At home: Outside 18
At school 20
Limiting waste 22

Glossary 23

Index 24